Unspoken

Unspoken

Poetry
by
Sharon Harris

Copyright 2011 Sharon Harris
All rights reserved

Published by
The Jackpine Writers' Bloc
13320 149th Ave
Menahga, MN 56464
sharrick1@wcta.net
www.jackpinewriters.com/sh

Printed in the United States of America

Cover photography by Sharon Harris
Cover and book design
by Tarah L. Wolff

ISBN: 978-1-928690-18-4

A person's best dreams,
deepest fears,
and worst hurts

often remain

Unspoken . . .

POETRY BOOKS BY SHARON HARRIS

Timeless Tracks
Life Savors
Unspoken

Acknowledgments

Grateful acknowledgment is made to the following magazines and journals for the previous publication of these poems:

American Press: "Pain," "Whirlpool"
County Lines: "Life-Worn"
Dust & Fire: "After the Funeral," "So Many Pieces"
Editor's Desk: "Aching," "Center of My Being"
The Edge: "Come Back Again"
LakesAlive: "Value Hidden"
Lucidity: "Another Day," "Lies," "Someone's Hands"
Moccasin: "Before You Came"
Natchez: "Room For You"
Odessa Poetry Review: "Precision"
PRHS Website: "The Present"
P&S Publishing: "Afterward"
Pen to Paper: "Bittersweet Rush"
Pilot Independent: "Hidden"
So. Poetry Magazine: "Adrift," "Knives"

Talking Stick: "Alzheimer's," "Car Accident," "Choices," "Circle of Vision," "The Empty End of Things," "The Funeral Procession," "Junk Mail," "Morning Glory," "Mother to Child," "Next Move," "Stop the Clock," "The Stroke," "Time Swirls Around Us," "Walking These Hills," "Will You Know?," "Revealed," "The Chances I Never Took," "How," "Reality," "Someday There Will be a Time," "Storm Coming," "Unaware," "Utter Loneliness," "What a Waste," "Will You Stay?," "Life-Worn," "New Reflections," "Winter Cover-Up," "Just One More," "Yearning"

Women's Stories: "Bittersweet Rush"

Yes Press: "Used to You"

Table of Contents

	PAGE
SEARCHING THROUGH THE SHADOWS	1
After the Funeral	3
Alzheimer's	4
Car Accident	5
Choices	6
Circle of Vision	7
The Empty End of Things	9
The Funeral Procession	10
Junk Mail	11
Morning Glory	12
Mother to Child	13
Next Move	14
Precision	15
The Present	16
Stop the Clock	17
The Stroke	18
Time Swirls Around Us	19
Walking These Hills	21
LIFETIMES	23
Ahead on the Path (for P.)	25
Come Back Again	26
If I Should Die	27
It's Time to Go	28
Last Breath	29
Will you Know?	31

Table of Contents

	PAGE
FANTASY (for P.)	33
Aching	35
Adrift	36
Afterward	37
Another Day	38
Before You Came	39
A Brittle Smile	40
Center of My Being	41
Flood	42
Knives	43
Lies	44
Pain	45
Revealed	46
Room for You	47
So Many Pieces	48
Someone's Hands	49
Whirlpool	50
STOLEN HEART (for R.)	51
Bittersweet Rush	53
The Chances I Never Took	54
How	55
It Was You	56
Reality	57
Someday There Will Be a Time	58
Storm Coming	59
Unaware	60
Used to You	61
Utter Loneliness	62
Value Hidden	63
What a Waste	64
Will You Stay?	65

Table of Contents

	PAGE	
NATURE'S MAGIC	67	
Four Seasons Women		69
Gypsy, Black Lab	71	
Just a Cat	72	
Life-Worn	73	
New Reflections	74	
Remaining Image	75	
Scamper	76	
Vision at Night	78	
Winter Cover-Up	79	
LOVE SONGS	81	
Hidden	83	
Just One More		84
Yearning	85	

Unspoken

SEARCHING THROUGH THE SHADOWS

After the Funeral

I spent the day
with tears sliding down my
   face
my throat aching
from holding back
the wrenching sobs

the funeral
finally ended
with a gun salute
and the folding
of the flag
at the graveyard

we breathed the same breath
and left marks on each other
needing to touch life deeply
and drink from it
and not feel so alone
trying hard to remind ourselves
that we still
have some time left

I should have gone
with the family
and smiled bravely
and helped serve lunch

instead
I grabbed
the best-looking man
in sight
and took him
home with me

Alzheimer's

the fog slips in
on little cat feet—

no, no, that's been done before.
rather let's say that
cotton candy cobwebs
drift in from the lake
to clutch at the edges of my vision.

mist or fog,
smoke or smog,
or a combination
of them all—
what is it?

it slides around me
with choking closeness,
slinks into my mind
with its cloying moist silence.

it is so hard to think—
what is it?
insanity, depression,
indecision,
or plain and simple confusion?

Car Accident

you suddenly
have nowhere you can go,
nowhere you can hide.
it is so in-your-face,
blotting out the rest of the world,
no choices,
no options.

when it is done,
and the crashing metal has stopped
reverberating
in your ears,

no matter what you had planned
for the day,
abruptly,
you have a whole new agenda.

Choices

I walk the rows
of tombstones and grave markers
and come to the place I chose to leave you,
the place I marked with a stone.

I sit awash in memories;
you're not really here, I know.
this body left here
is only the shell your spirit used
while on this earth.

how much better it might have been
to let fire consume you
down to the barest particles of existence

and keep you at home near me
and near your favorite things,
perhaps on a shelf surrounded by your books,
your papers.

how much better yet it might have been
to let those ashes fly far and free
to someday grow again

in some new blade of grass or tree
reaching up from the earth
into the blueness
and endless reaches
      of sky.

Circle of Vision

when
you start out
in this life
your world
is so small

the circle
of your mother's arms
is all that is clear
the rest of your surroundings
are fuzzy, unimaginable

they gradually clear
and expand to your crib,
your room, your house,
later on, the yard, the street,
a school, a job

for a while your world encompasses so much
the circle you control is so wide
the world you can explore seems so open and endless
so full of possibilities

>>>

Unspoken

now old
and crippled
and eyesight failing
the circle of your vision
decreases
your world shrinks again
to narrow reality
down to just
your house,
your room,
your bed,
the circle
of a loved one's arms

The Empty End of Things

I am really
feeling
the empty end
of things

I see gravity
spoiling
my lines
when once
I felt
beautiful

I feel
my age
my childlessness
the absence
of family

I see
my inability
to change anything

but mostly
I still
just feel
the loss
of you

The Funeral Procession

stopped at the graveside.
people stood
in hushed respect
and held each other
while the minister droned.

cars roared by
and birds sang
and the wind blew
and grass grew
and children played and laughed.

we had stopped for death
but all around us
life went on

while a spirit
slipped away. . . .

Junk Mail

I gather my mail
from the box
and sort through it
in an irritated fashion

junk mail
ads for credit cards
stuff I will never open
my trash barrel
eats it up

I check my email
on the computer
and sort through it
in an irritated fashion

junk email
ads for credit cards
and sexual aids
hints of pornographic
pleasures
at the click of a button
my delete key
eats them up

later I go visit my aging mother

so alone and lonely
nothing brightens days
that are already dim
due to diminished eyesight

she pleads,
"any mail today
for me?"

Morning Glory

my mom and I
plant
one packet
of morning glory seeds
every spring

it is our unfailing
ritual
something we do together
every year

she is ninety-three
I worry and wonder
how many more springs
we will get to do this

in the store today
I spotted a display
of flower seeds

in sudden desperation
I plucked ten or twelve packets
of morning glories
from the shelf
and hurried to buy them

Mother to Child

I feel like
you are my heart
now outside
of my body

somehow when
you were born
my heart
became you

I will never
feel whole again
unless
I am
holding you

Next Move

huddled over

the chessboard

of my life,

I ponder

my next move

Precision

you
ask me
why I am so precise
why I make lists
and keep records
why I must keep track
    of all my details.

why do you ask?
can't you see?
isn't it plain to you
the perfect cycle of the seasons
the ceaseless movements of the stars
the rhythmic precision of tides and winds
the planets in their predictable orbits?

isn't it natural
that I too
must keep record of my details?
that I too
must keep my plotted course?

Unspoken

The Present

we go through life

eating up our future

in great gulps

turning it

so quickly

into our past

Stop the Clock

stop the clock!
turn its face to the wall.
there!
I've stopped time!
I don't have to worry anymore;
I can do what I want,
I don't have to hurry.

but no!
I've only lost track of it.
even now I can feel it
sneaking by.
I can hear its passing
like the wind howling around
the corner of a building,
like the sound you hear
with your ear to the phone—
the sound of distance whining,
when no one's talking on the line.

The Stroke

my poor father,
once the life of the party;
now the spark
has gone out
of his eyes.

that smile
that used to light up
a room
now is feeble,
bent.

Dad,
you have been broken
and put back
together
wrong;
you are not
the same.

is the best part
of you
floating above
us all
waiting for
total release?

are you just
waiting,
wondering
why we won't
let go?

Time Swirls Around Us

my poor father
now old and bent
a stroke has changed him
he drifts in and out of reality

sometimes on a sunny day
when the sky is clear and so is he
he will ask me to take him for a walk
down the driveway
from the house where he has lived so long

slowly, laboriously, he hobbles
clutching his cane in one good hand
head bent
watching each foot slowly respond
and move ahead at his command

I walk patiently at his side
one hand on his belt
ready to catch him if he falls

time swirls around us like the wind
it sweeps the leaves around us
and blows them across our path

suddenly, surely, I can see
embedded in this driveway
our tracks from fifty years ago

>>>

Unspoken

a vision comes to me
when we walked this same path
my feet then were small and unsure

and he was in his prime
walking beside me
proud and tall
ready to catch me if I should fall

Walking These Hills

he chose this land.
his family came
from far away.
he learned its hills
and hollows;
he cleared the land
and reaped a harvest
and raised a family
and smiled
every day.

now he's gone,
attached to all of us
yet not quite here.

in his funeral caravan
we pass by the old place;
his spirit is floating with us.
how silly for us to mourn
when he is everywhere
around us
still walking these hills
and hollows
with a smile
as wide
as the sky.

LIFETIMES

Ahead on the Path
(for P.)

my heart reaches out to you
gentle friend
in your loss
and your sorrow.

there's a big hole in your heart,
isn't there?
it must take your breath away.

please let my thoughts and words
help to heal that wound in your heart.
please feel the big hug
I'm mentally sending you.

the sweet history
between us
makes me feel your pain
like it was mine.
if it helps at all,
please know that I share it.

please know that your brother
is not gone—
he is just ahead of you
on the path.

someday when it's your time to go,
you will round a corner
and he'll be there,
with your dad,
waiting for you. . . .

Come Back Again

the good things always come back
if you give them time

spring comes back
       around again
after endless winter

flowers spring
       up again
from dead stalks and frozen roots

my dad
whose great heart I have sorely missed
shows up again
in the laughing eyes
of my baby nephew

If I Should Die

if I should die
unexpectedly,
please know that I did not mind going.

of course I will miss you,
all my loved ones;
of course I will miss the earth,
this sweep of sky,
this stretch of stars.
of course I will miss the things
I did not finish.

but I know that I have other places to be,
other things to do.
and I know that I will return someday
and share times with you again.
look for me in the wind,
look for me in a sunset.
look for me in the eyes
of a newborn babe;
I will never be far from you.

if I should die
unexpectedly,
please know that I did not mind going.

It's Time to Go

when these bodies
have carried us
as far as they can,

and, like faithful steeds,
are put down,

our energy,
the real "us,"
rises
and floats and flies—

time to
move on,
no longer
weighed down
by
earthly
cares

Last Breath

I floated up
and examined the ceiling
and the light fixtures—
not sure what I was doing there—

I knew that I could pass right through it all
if I wanted to
but I was content
to waft in the air
like a feather

then I looked down
puzzled
my daughters sat by a hospital bed
looking so shaken and tearful
next to a shrunken version of me

how silly, how trivial
I wish I could tell them
I am just fine
floating far and free
slowly unraveling from that life

let me go, my children
I enjoyed every breath
of life that I had
and I smiled every day

but the body you wait by
is just a shell
that I wore
while I was there

>>>

Unspoken

the love continues
but the body ends

and I have other things
to attend to now
it is time to let me go
and just know
that I am fine
floating far and free

and yet
right beside you

Will You Know?

when I die
will you know?

somewhere far away,
will you turn
from what you are doing?
will you wonder
what
you felt

when I touch you,
sliding by
on my way
to forever?

FANTASY
(for P.)

Aching

today
I am aching
today
I am hurting

there are so many things
I need to say
so many things
I need to tell you
so many ways
I need to touch you

please. . .
can't you be here
with me?

Adrift

I feel
like I'm floating adrift
in uncharted waters

watching for shoreline
hoping for wind
hoping for light

with very little control
over my life

Afterward

I am always surprised
    afterward
that your fingerprints
don't show on my skin

in a telling pattern
leaving a message
for all to see

changing me
for all to notice

saying to the world
    in bold print:

I have touched this lady!
I have loved her!
she is mine!

Another Day

I came home late
exhausted
hoping to fall
into the blissful
    oblivion
     of sleep

I cross another day
off on the calendar—
another day
    I've survived
    without you

Fantasy

Before You Came

my life
is a pile
of abandoned dreams and visions
that once were
>so important.

my life
is a heap
>of discarded hopes and plans
that once were
>all that mattered.

A Brittle Smile

a short visit to the dentist:
I went in sober with a brittle smile.
I drifted away on a cloud of gas and Novocain
meant to relax me, to eliminate my pain.
the pain still touched me
but my mind sailed away
and inside I let go
and inside I was screaming your name
and the words I love you
and I want to tell you I love you
and I will die without you
won't there ever be anything for us?

I cried inside my mind
I called to you
I cried and screamed your name
inside my head
as I floated far away.

the dentist did his job
the gas was switched to oxygen
and I came down slowly
my mind cleared
and composed and smiling a brittle smile
I went out sober.

Fantasy

Center of My Being

YOU

are my light,

my sun,

the quiet stillness

at the center of my being.

Flood

I saw you unexpectedly today
with her

a flood of pain
was unleashed
and went splashing uncontrollably
inside my head
a dull roar filled
my ears with torment

and I closed my eyes
and just sat quietly
with no one even noticing
as I silently drowned
in a tidal wave
of memories

Fantasy

Knives

a hundred

little knives

of memory

are stabbing me

today

with every breath

I take

Lies

if I
could only
turn a knob
or push a button
and shut
off my mind

it keeps
playing my memories
like a movie—
visions of
us together
in our best moments
touching and loving

it keeps
playing your words
like a song—
your caressing loving voice
touching me like silk
your smooth sentences
wrapping me in lies

Pain

there's a lot of pain
    behind my eyes
that you can't see
    because I'm hiding it
with smiles and laughter
    and brave words.

oh, let my whole life pass
    smooth and creamy
the way today did
    next to you.

don't you see that I'd rather have
    a little bit of you
now and then
    rather than none of you
    at all?

Revealed

peeling apples
in my kitchen
watching the jewel-red
        circular stripes
        falling away
from the edge of my paring knife
        revealing the firm white flesh beneath

reminds me
of how
with sure fingers
you uncovered me
and took away my shyness
and insecurities
        along with my clothes

and revealed the real me
naked, clean
and trembling
ready for the first heart-stopping touch
of your lips

Fantasy

Room for You

I had
never planned
on meeting you

you took me
by surprise

I had to make room
for you
in my life

I had to move aside
some needless details
and shove aside
some boring cumbersome
trivia
that was cluttering
my life

only filling up
time and space
till you came

So Many Pieces

waking up again
with my arms
around a stranger—

hung over and
half-sick and
delirious—
with memories
of the night before
full of black holes—

I am so broken
into so many
bitter, resentful pieces
that even if you
came back,
I don't think you
could put me
back together again
the way
I was.

Fantasy

Someone's Hands

I saw someone's hands
that reminded me of yours.

out with a group of friends
sipping a drink
suddenly someone's hands—
        like yours, came into view.

then, all I could see was
a flash of your fingers
    reaching for me,
touching me the way you do,
    stroking my thighs. . .

sick with longing, limp with desire,
I smile and chat quietly with my friends
while all the time
    I'm watching floating visions
        of your hands, your fingers,
    caressing me, holding me. . .

Whirlpool

I am
caught
constantly
in a whirlpool
of emotions

I am
pulled
down
by a fierce undertow

the eddies
and currents
of memories of you
keep pulling me under

I can't
keep my head
above water
and concentrate
on living

STOLEN HEART
(for R.)

Bittersweet Rush

the old house still stands at the water's edge.
loon calls still echo down the length of the lake
    in the darkness.
the sky still burnishes the water to pink and gold
    at dusk
    like it always did.

a familiar screen door's slam calls to mind
    a million old memories,
brings back a bittersweet rush of faces, words,
    feelings, sights, and sounds.

in the yard, dead trees are a child's hands
    reaching mute fingers
    to an uncaring sky.

some things stay the same;
some things change totally and are gone forever.

it should be that all good things could be chosen
    to remain the same,
    permanent like sky and water
and all the bad haunting things should disappear
    as easily
    as morning mist
    on the lake.

The Chances I Never Took

what a strange feeling,
meeting him by chance
after so many years have gone by.

I let him go without me
wherever the roads would lead him.
I chose safety and security
and places I already knew.

I place my hand now against his cheek
and let my eyes tell him my regrets,
let my eyes tell him of my love
that never died, words I still cannot speak.

in his eyes
I see all the places I never saw,
all the things I never did,
all the chances I never took.

How

thoughts from each of us
silent in the dark
but vibrating, needing to be spoken

I'm sure he wonders
how he traversed the whole world
staying free
and ended up here with me
tying him down

and I wonder
how my careful little existence
my tight little world—that rarely
      let anyone in—
let in this dark outlaw
sure to steal my heart
and disappear
as swiftly
as he appeared

It Was You

I had a dream
and in my dream I searched
for lost youth and beauty
and strolled into a room
and said to myself
I want to find someone
who is attracted to me
as I am now
and someone I will be attracted to

I strolled and nodded and smiled
and some gentleman
slipped his arm around me
and I only saw the back of his head
as he finished speaking
to someone else

nice looking
plenty of hair
great suit

and he turned

and it was you
of course
it was you

Reality

my mind
is spinning
with thoughts
and feelings.

my ears
are ringing
on a flat plain
of silence.

my head
is a vacuum.

my throat aches
with tears to be shed,
words to be said.

I never dreamed
you would leave me.

Storm Coming

we used to stand
in the open doorway
of the garage
and watch the storm
tear apart the sky
we shuddered at the thunder
and flinched at the lightning
and stood in awe
at the rush of water

now you call me
you in your home
me in mine
a separation
I will never understand

you mention a storm
better get off the phone
you say

what happened to your nerve
your recklessness
we used to kiss in the open garage door
daring lightning to reach us
you would take me by the hand
and pull me into the back seat
of our car in the garage
and we would make love
to the crashing of the storm
and the rush of the rain
while our neighbors
drove by
unknowing

Someday There Will be a Time

someday
there will be a time
when I will not think of you
when a storm rages
and thunder booms
and lightning fractures the sky

someday
there will be a time
when I will not wear you
wrapped
like barbed wire
around my heart

Unspoken

Unaware

life

took us apart

when

we weren't

looking

Used to You

just when I'd gotten used to you being there
just when I'd gotten used to reaching for you
in the night
just when I had adjusted to your breathing
to the contours of your body and your night sounds
just when I got to depend on you

your turned away from me
you left me
feeling so lost
endlessly reaching for you
in the night

Utter Loneliness

seeking to get, needing to get closer
losing yourself in the passion
needing so much to get inside that other person
to merge, to share, to lose that awful aloneness
becoming one
needing that, craving that,
momentarily losing yourself in the feeling
of not being alone

afterward
when the lovemaking is done
you look around, you look out the window
and down the road
you can feel nothing now
but that utter loneliness
settling back on you
back with all its smothering baggage
back with those awful childhood memories
all laying heavily about your shoulders again
falling back into place
closing off your heart
and your mind

Value Hidden

when I see a candy treat
    all wrapped up in cellophane
a sweet treasure
    just waiting to be opened

I think of you
    look at what you could be
thinking you are nothing
when all the world but you
    can see
        the value hidden in your heart

What A Waste

I get through the days okay
busy at work
rushing home
chores to do
my pets to care for
I even treasure the evening time alone
the remote is mine
everything is in its place
the silence in the house
de-stresses me
from the busy-ness of the day

but every single time
I tuck myself in at night
I think of you
alone in your big house
as I am alone in mine
and my heart hurts
and I think
what a waste of a life
spending it away
from the person you love most

Will You Stay?

looking back through years of faces,
    feelings, words
I still see your face before all others
clearer than the rest
and nearer, dearer to my heart

as long as you are on this earth
I know I cannot see beyond you

when you are eighty
and done running
will you finally come back to me?
when you have tasted all the world
    has to offer
will you finally know that the best part
    was what you left behind?

will you sit down with me before the fire
    and hold my hand
and will you stay, finally?

NATURE'S MAGIC

Nature's Magic

Four Seasons Women
1. Spring

Spring
is a fiery maiden
with a dare-you look in her eyes,
with a come-on in the sway of her body
when she walks,
when she dances,
with a vibrant soulful beauty in her voice
when she sings.
there's a great heat about her,
a voluptuousness that can't go unnoticed.
celebration and joy are her companions.
she gives to them all her warmth and her love.
she is hot nights and burning stars,
flaming moon and smoldering rain,
a flower in sunlit glory.

2. Summer

Summer
is a lovely lady,
warm and tender,
changing from moments of hot passion
to moments of coolness.
she loves to float for endless hours
in a canoe on a lake;
her skin is sun-bronzed,
her hair sun-bleached and golden.
she rises early in the morning
with her eyes opening
like summer flowers to the sun.
she dances far into the night
lovely, warm and gentle
like a soft summer rainfall.   >>>

3. Autumn

Autumn
is a shy lady,
gentle and cool,
a bit aloof in her ways,
sharp sometimes
but beautiful too.
she dresses in robes of brilliant color,
ever-changing
from rust to gold,
from amber to shimmering red.
she is flamboyant in her dress
but quiet otherwise.
there is a deep secrecy in her voice,
frost on her breath
and the look of death in her eyes.

4. Winter

Winter
is an icy woman.
she swathes herself in white gowns
with ermine collars
and high silver boots.
her hair hangs dark and lifeless,
her eyes have a hungry, haunted look.
she is so pale.
her eyes are listless
her fingers,
long and thin,
are blue with cold.
she has never known warmth;
she must go her way alone,
a frigid lonely lady.

Nature's Magic

Gypsy, Black Lab

I'll never forget
holding her
as she breathed
her last breath
and heaved a big sigh
and left us.

as we lay in bed
that night
I was so aware
that she now lay
permanently,
not too far from our window,
beside the path
she used to run on.

a storm broke
and rain poured down.
lightning flashed
and the thunderclaps that shook the sky
were her growls,
her angry protests
against losing the life
she enjoyed
and leaving the people
she loved.

Just a Cat

after all, he's just a cat.

those words enrage me.
he might be just a cat,
but he's been here
when you haven't been.

he's been
my most faithful friend.
the louder I cried,
the louder he purred.
when I fell apart,
he stayed with me.

he's been right here
when you haven't been.

after all, you're just a man.

Life-Worn

the old dog,
with several strokes behind her,
has lived more lives
than most cats.

she stands
at the corner
of her kennel
with aching joints.

her near-blind eyes
stare at the forest's edge.
she woofs quietly
at even intervals,
life-worn,

calling death,
asking the peaceful darkness
to come for her.

New Reflections

spring came
while I spent the day inside.

going out
in early evening,
expecting dingy snow banks,

I was startled
by the perfect reflection
of the sky
in a new puddle
in my driveway.

Nature's Magic

Remaining Image

I was startled awake one morning,
leaping to my feet.
grinding roaring sounds
came from my neighbor's forest
close to me.

I looked out my window
and watched big machines cutting trees—
trees that have stood there for years,
fighting their own battles to survive,
harming no one.
imagine how long it took
for them to grow so tall.

I fled.
I could watch no more.
too late—
the image remained with me—
I had watched in mute, helpless horror
as a big machine
grasped a tall mature pine
in its jaws.

the saw began
and in its last moments
the tree shook
and trembled—
the top of it flailing violently—

waving its last goodbye
to the sky.

Scamper

my black cat
with white feet and chest
you look like you are wearing
a tuxedo

you always are so full of love
you've seen me through so much
times I've cried and screamed my heartbreak
      to the skies
you've sat in my lap
and purred on and on
you are my rock
the only thing to hold me to earth
      and to sanity

you understood
you absorbed it all
you helped to ease the pain
you purred your continuous
      unending unchanging song
telling me that life goes on
some things are constant
but pain will go away
      or diminish
and love continues

you reached out one white paw
      with those silly pink toes
and patted my face
as I rocked and cried

                                                             >>>

Nature's Magic

you were just always there
steady and solid, steady in your love,
you do not change, you do not have moods
all you want is love
and you give so much in return

your big golden eyes
    always saw everything
that went on in this house
    and you never told on me
sometimes I hardly said a word to you
    rushing in and out
but when I needed you
    you were always there

lovers come and lovers go
and you have watched them all
through those half-closed golden eyes

you knew that
sooner or later
we'd be left here alone again

you're the only faithful one. . .

Vision at Night

driving
a country road
at night
snow piled deep
in the ditches

turning a corner,
my headlights
flash far across
a frozen field

capturing for an instant
the glowing eyes of many deer
clustered like the lights
of a tiny village
far away in the dark

Winter Cover-Up

snow melts,
the big banks shrink
in the ditches,
revealing
all kinds
of unsavory things
that winter had hidden.

a rib cage
of a deer
reaches up
like mute fingers
to an uncaring sky—
frozen delicacy
for neighborhood dogs.

LOVE SONGS

Hidden

fog surrounds me,
swirling against my skin.
it covers the lake
and hides the road,
conceals the ground
in front of me.

silence
cloaks my soul,
shields me from you—
you who say you love me.
but you do not know me
and cannot see the real me
walking all over your heart.

Just One More

how desperate
I am
not to be over

not to be
done yet

there
must be room
in this heart

and time
in this life

for one more
great love

Yearning

I sit in a coffee shop,
alone
but not by choice,

missing you
and not far enough
from funeral arrangements
to remember just the good things,

feeling my age,
while steam
drifts up from my cup.

idly I watch
as a young boy
comes in with his girl.

they are new to each other,
I can tell,
unsure what to say
and how to say it,
blushing but smiling
broadly at each other.

oh, to be that young,
to have it all start again—
that first blush of love,
the promise
of a whole long life
still ahead of us.

www.ingramcontent.com/pod-product-compliance
Lightning Source LLC
Chambersburg PA
CBHW060402050426
42449CB00009B/1857